Florence A Bermuda Story

Easter Sunday 1953

Florence A Bermuda Story
Easter Sunday 1953

A Short Story by:

Juliet D Wilkinson

ISBN: 978-1-957724-13-3 (Paperback Edition)
ISBN: 978-1-957724-12-6 (Hardcover Edition)
ISBN: 978-1-957724-14-0 (E-book Edition)

Book Ordering Information

The Regency Publishers, US
521 5th Ave 17th floor NY, NY10175
Phone Number: (315)537-3088 ext 1007
Email: info@theregencypublishers.com
www.theregencypublishers.com

Printed in the United States of America

Contents

Foreword...1

Special Thanks..3

Florence A Bermuda Story................................5

One Documentary Titled 38

FOREWORD

TO MY ANCESTORS

I GIVE HOMAGE TO YOU FOR
INSTILLING YOUR STRENGTH,

COURAGE, COMPASSION, HUMILITY,
INTEGRITY HARD WORK WITH A

SONG IN YOUR SPIRIT INTO MY
GRANDPARENTS, WHO HAS PASSED IT

ONTO THEIR CHILDREN AND
THEIR CHILDREN'S CHILDREN

GIVE THANKS TO THE CREATOR

SPECIAL THANKS

TO MY MOM, AUNT FRANCES,
AND MY AUNT MYRTLE FOR
CONFIRMING THE STORIES THAT
MY GRANDPARENTS TOLD ME.

MY DAUGHTER RAYNETTE, FOR ALL
HER HELP WITH PUTTING THIS
BOOK TOGETHER.

MS. KENISHA SHAKIR FROM THE
BERMUDA NATIONAL LIBRARY FOR
ALL HER HELP WITH COLLECTING
THE ROYAL GAZETTE DIGITAL
FILES ON THE TORNADOES THAT
HIT BERMUDA IN APRIL 1953.

FLORENCE A BERMUDA STORY

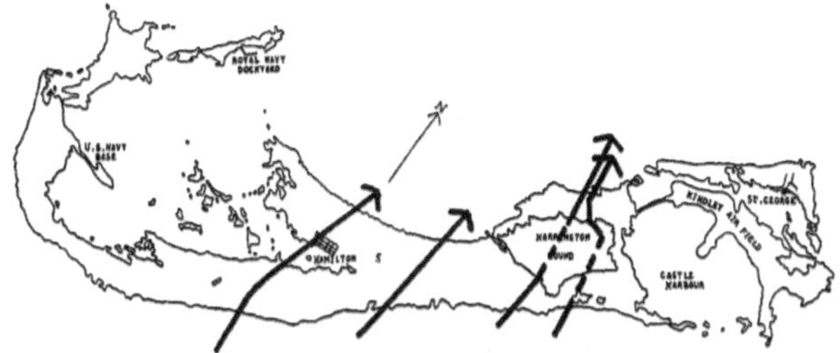

The Easter Tornadoes at Bermuda

W. A. Macky, *Bermuda Meteorological Service*

THE central part of Bermuda was visited by at least four tornadoes between 1800 and 1830 on Easter Sunday, 5 April 1953. Moving from south to north across the narrow island, the twisters did considerable damage to property, killed one woman, and caused many injuries ranging from minor bruises to broken limbs.

The two most westerly tracks shown on the accompanying map were reasonably well defined, but there is some doubt about the others. It appears that the westernmost tornado came in from the sea about 1806, the middle two about 1815, and the easternmost about 1820. All observers state that they looked like a heavy rain squall and did not have the sharply defined boundaries of typical waterspouts. Several people reported that they could see the cloud rotating, and many felt a sudden pressure change in their ears. Heavy continuous lightning occurred in the central two but not in the others.

The westernmost whirl passed very close to the meteorological office where the anemometer recorded two gusts to 89 and 85 mph at about 1812. At this time the barograph trace fell about eight millibars and rose again immediately to a higher value than before. The record shows that the wind veered from northeast to west at the moment of the two extreme gusts.

On the weather map, a depression was located about 150 miles west of Bermuda at 1400 with a warm front approaching the island group from the southwest. Weather had been overcast with low clouds during the day, and intermittent rain fell during the afternoon. The wind from the southsoutheast increased to 28 mph by 1700, and a very heavy rain fell in most parts of Bermuda about 1800, with one inch in 15 minutes being recorded at Hamilton. The surface warm front passed at this time, and apparently the tornadoes were associated with the passage.

About 90 properties were damaged, but only a few buildings were so demolished that they became uninhabitable. In most cases the damage consisted of sucking or blowing from the roofs the slates of Bermuda stone, with which all island structures are traditionally covered, leaving the supporting wooden rafters intact.

The most spectacular damage was on the south side of Harrington Sound where the tornado came down from the higher land and picked up several poultry coops containing hundreds of chickens which vanished entirely, apparently into the water. At the same time the twister lifted one parked car and another that was moving on the road, depositing them in the sea right side up about 100 feet away. Fortunately, the occupied car stayed afloat long enough for the driver to escape.

There were many instances of adjacent

7

The damage caused by the sucking aloft of the roof stones of a Bermuda house is illustrated in this scene of destruction.

objects being carried in opposite directions and of articles of clothing being sucked through the ceiling of unroofed houses. In Hamilton a gentleman standing on his verandah saw a large beach umbrella fly past from the east. Then, perhaps 15 seconds later, the wind blew straight in from the south piling debris on his verandah, and, a few seconds later, the umbrella flew past again coming from the west.

Heavy objects were blown considerable distances, and there would probably have been a much heavier toll of life but for the facts that the day was a Sunday and that the heavy rain beforehand had driven people to take shelter indoors. The one casualty resulted when a woman left a damaged house to carry her small sister to safety and was struck by flying debris while the baby was unhurt.

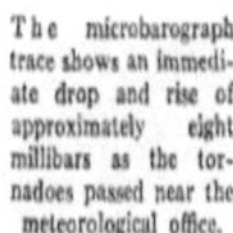

The microbarograph trace shows an immediate drop and rise of approximately eight millibars as the tornadoes passed near the meteorological office.

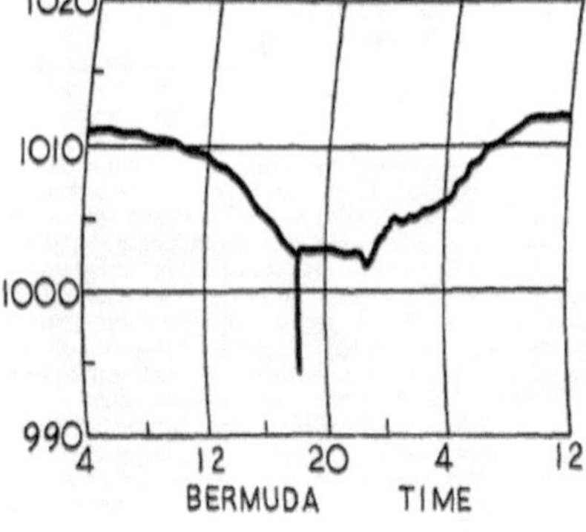

8

FLORENCE AND PERCY SMITH

THIS IS A STORY OF THE SMITH FAMILY, THE LATE PERCY SMITH, BORN OCTOBER 31/1907, DIED OCTOBER 28/ 1983.

THE LATE FLORENCE WILKINSON SMITH, BORN AUGUST 11/1908, DIED JULY 17/ 1998

PERCY WAS FROM HARRIS BAY SMITHS PARISH AND FLORENCE WAS FROM BAILEY'S BAY HAMILTON PARISH.

PERCY MADE HIS LIVING AS A FISHERMAN AND HE LOVED BEING AT SEA. FLORENCE WAS A DOMESTIC WORKER AND WORKED FOR MANY WEALTHY PEOPLE IN TUCKERS TOWN. SHE ALSO ACCOMPANIED THEM SEVERAL TIMES TO THE USA. ALL WHILE RAISING A FAMILY OF EIGHT, FIVE GIRLS AND THREE BOYS.

LIFE WAS VERY HARD IN THE EARLY DAYS IN BERMUDA FOR ITS BLACK POPULATION.

FLORENCE WAS A VERY STRICT NO-NONSENSE HARD-WORKING WOMAN. THEY WERE BOTH THE PRODUCT

OF AFRIKAN, THE FIRST PEOPLE OF THE AMERICAS, AND EUROPEAN HERITAGE.

FLORENCE WAS A TALL BLACK WOMAN WITH LONG STRAIGHT BLACK HAIR FLOWING DOWN TO HER WAIST.

I LOVED TO HEAR THE STORIES THAT MY GRANDFATHER WOULD TELL ME OF HOW HE FELL IN LOVE WITH MY GRANDMOTHER.

HE FIRST SAW HER WHEN SHE WAS ABOUT FOURTEEN YEARS OLD. SHE WAS IN A HORSE AND BUGGY ALONG WITH A MEMBER OF THE WHITE WILKINSON FAMILY TRAVELING ALONG THE HARRINGTON SOUND ROAD NEAR DEVIL'S HOLE.

WHAT CAUGHT HIS EYES WAS THIS BEAUTIFUL BLACK GIRL SITTING IN THE HORSE AND BUGGY WITH FLOWING JET-BLACK HAIR FLYING IN THE WIND. FOR HIM IT WAS LOVE AT FIRST SIGHT.

HE FOUND OUT THAT SHE WAS A BAILEY'S BAY GIRL, AND HE FELT THAT HE MAY NOT STAND A CHANCE WITH HER, FOR THE GIRLS FROM BAILEY'S BAY WERE KNOWN TO BE VERY SAUCIE, AND TRUE TO FORM SHE WAS.

THEY WERE MARRIED AT A VERY YOUNG AGE. ONE OF MY GREATEST JOYS IN LIFE WAS SPENDING TIME WITH MY GRANDPARENTS.

THE VERY FIRST CIRCUS THAT I EVER WENT TO WAS WITH THEM. MY GRANDMOTHER'S NICKNAME FOR ME WAS "LITTLE MOUSE". SHE HAD NICKNAMES FOR ALL OF HER EIGHT CHILDREN.

MY GRANDMOTHER NEVER LEARNED TO READ OR WRITE. HER SIGNATURE WAS AN "X" BUT AS A LITTLE CHILD I WOULD SEE HER ALWAYS HAVING A NEWSPAPER IN HER HANDS DAILY! AND TELLING ME WHAT WAS IN THE PAPER?

AND WHENEVER SHE WENT TO THE GROCERY SHOP, SHE ALWAYS PAID FOR HER PRODUCTS WITH THE RIGHT AMOUNT OF CASH.

IT WAS NOTHING THAT SHE COULD NOT DO, FROM TAKING OUT HER LITTLE PUNT INTO THE HARRINGTON SOUND TO CATCH FISH, DIVE FOR MUSSELS AND LOBSTERS, MAKING CLOTHES FOR HER CHILDREN TO WEAR, AS WELL AS RIDING HER MOTORBIKE AROUND THE ISLAND.

ON HER BUSY DAY, SHE WAS THE FAMILY DOCTOR. ANY AILMENTS THAT THE FAMILY OR HER NEIGHBOURS HAD, SHE WOULD MAKE AN HERBAL CURE. I CAN STILL SEE THE BIG STAINLESS STEEL POT ON HER STOVE, WITH A LARGE ROCKFISH HEAD BEING BOILED DOWN. AS SHE MADE FISH CHOWDER, THE SMELL STILL LINGERS WITH ME TO THIS DAY.

HER FAMOUS BERMUDA SHARK HASH, SERVED WITH HOPPING JOHN'S AND RICE SWEET POTATO AND PUMPKIN. NO ONE MADE SHARK HASH LIKE MY GRANDMOTHER AND TO SPEAK OF HER CASSAVA PIE.

I REMEMBER WHEN MY GRANDMOTHER WOULD COME TO MY SCHOOL FRANCIS PATTON PRIMARY, IN HAMILTON PARISH TO BRING ME SOME FRESH BAKED GOODIES, THE CHILDREN WOULD SAY, HERE COMES JULIET'S GRANDMOTHER "BLACK GERONIMO" RIDING HER HORSE, "IT WAS HER MOTORBIKE".

BEING A CHILD, I WAS HURT BY THEM CALLING HER THAT, NOT KNOWING THAT IT WAS PART OF MY HERITAGE, SOMETHING FOR ME TO BE PROUD OF.

AS I LOOK BACK TO THAT TIME IN MY LIFE
THESE WORDS COME TO MIND, " OUT OF THE MOUTH OF BABES"
CHILDREN HAVE A SIMPLE WAY OF KNOWING THE TRUTH
JUST BY THEM LOOKING AT MY GRANDMOTHER,
THEY SAW THAT SHE WAS DIFFERENT, THEY SAW HER AS AN INDIAN, WHERE I JUST SAW MY GRANDMOTHER.

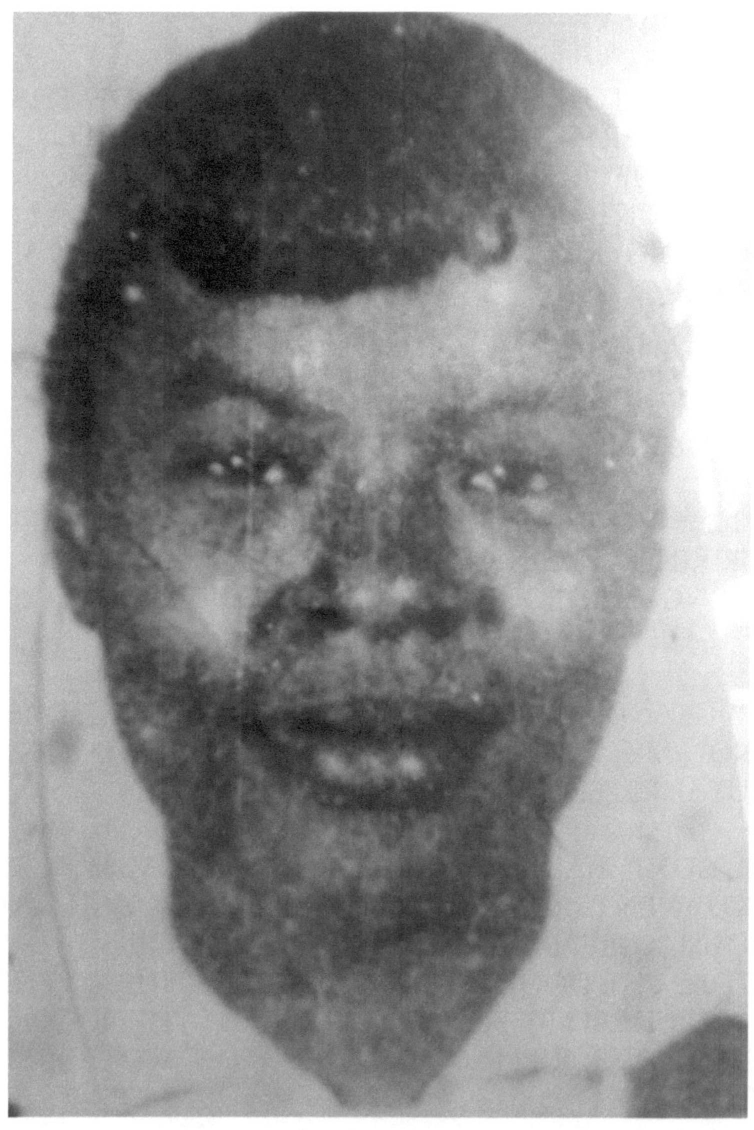

AUNT MADELINE

THIS STORY IS ABOUT WHAT MY GRANDMOTHER FLORENCE HAD TO ENDURE ON EASTER SUNDAY APRIL 5 1953.

AS TOLD TO ME BY HER AND MY GRANDFATHER, ON EASTER SUNDAY APRIL 5 1953, IT STARTED AS A BEAUTIFUL SUNNY DAY. MY GRANDFATHER, MY MOM, AUNT FRANCES, AND MY AUNT MYRTLE WERE WORKING. MY AUNT MADELINE WAS TAKING CARE OF ME.

OUT OF NOWHERE, A TORNADO APPEARED CROSSING THE HARRINGTON SOUND, PICKING UP CARS AND BIKES DROPPING THEM INTO THE WATER.

THEN IT TRAVELED TO ABBOTT'S CLIFF AREA STRIKING THE COTTAGE THAT THEY LIVED IN TAKING THE ROOF OF THE HOUSE AND CAUSING LOTS OF DAMAGE.

MY GRANDMOTHER GATHERED UP HER CHILDREN AND MY TWO BROTHERS TRYING TO SEEK OUT SHELTER.

MY AUNT MADELINE GRABBED ME FROM MY CRIB AND WENT RUNNING WITH ME THROUGH THE HOUSE SCREAMING TRYING TO GET OUT. SHE WAS HIT BY THE DOOR FLYING OPEN, THEN SHE WAS HIT IN HER HEAD BY FLYING SLATE FROM THE ROOF OF THE HOUSE, KILLING HER INSTANTLY, WITH ME IN HER ARMS.

THE TORNADO WITH ITS SWIRLING WINDS GATHERED ME UP TAKING ME TOWARDS THE FARM GARDENS. ON ABBOTT'S CLIFF, MY GRANDMOTHER HAD TO LEAVE

HER DAUGHTER TO RUN AFTER ME IN THE POURING RAIN AND HEAVY WINDS TO FIND ME.

THE TORNADO DROP ME IN THE BANANA PATCHES WHERE THE COWS WERE LAYING DOWN.

I WAS FOUND IN THE MIDST OF THE COWS. IT WAS A STORY THAT ALL OF MY COUSINS WOULD LOVE TO TELL IN SCHOOL DURING STORYTELLING TIME.

"SOME PEOPLE SAY THAT I WAS FOUND HIGH IN THE TREES" AND THAT MY GRANDMOTHER HAD TO CLIMB THE TREE TO GET ME. I THINK THAT SOME PEOPLE THOUGHT THAT I WAS KILLED ALSO.

"HOW IN HELL" WAS MY GRANDMOTHER WAS ABLE TO SAVE ME, PLUS GET SOMEONE TO TAKE CARE OF THE CHILDREN WHILE SHE WENT WITH MY AUNT MADELINE TO THE HOSPITAL.

THE MOST HEARTBREAKING PART OF THIS TRAGEDY WAS THAT MY AUNT MADELINE WAS PREGNANT AND DUE TO BE MARRIED WITHIN A COUPLE OF WEEKS.

SHE WAS BURIED IN HER WEDDING GOWN. THE GROOM TO BE THEY SAY WAS NEVER THE SAME AFTER THAT, HE WAS IN SO MUCH PAIN THAT HE LEFT BERMUDA NEVER TO RETURN.

THE HELL THAT MY GRANDMOTHER HAD TO ENDURE ON THAT EASTER SUNDAY DAY IS SOMETHING THAT SHE NEVER FORGOT.

AS I LISTEN TO HER TELLING ME HOW ON THAT TERRIBLE DAY, AS SHE HELD MY AUNT MADELINE IN

HER ARMS, SCREAMING FOR HELP, MR. HODGSON HER NEIGHBOUR PASSED HER BY, THEN RIGHT BEHIND HIM CAME YOUNG RANDOLPH FURBERT WHO QUICKLY WENT TO GET A CAR TO TAKE MY AUNT MADELINE TO THE HOSPITAL WHERE SHE WAS PRONOUNCED DEAD UPON ARRIVAL.

SHE THEN GOT A TAXI TO TAKE HER TO PINK BEACH CLUB TO PICK UP MY MOM THEN SHE TRAVELED TO TOM MOORE'S TAVERN TO PICK UP MY AUNT FRANCES AND MY AUNT MYRTLE.

IN SOME PLACES ON THE ISLAND, PEOPLE DID NOT KNOW THAT A TORNADO HAD HIT BERMUDA. WHEN THEY ARRIVED AT WHERE THEIR HOUSE ONCE STOOD, MY GRANDFATHER WAS THERE ALONG WITH MANY OF HIS FRIENDS OFFERING TO HELP.

IT WAS THE MOST HEARTBREAKING SCENE FOR THEM TO BEAR, AND TO KNOW THAT THEY HAD LOST THEIR BELOVED DAUGHTER MADELINE, AND THE CHILDREN HAD LOST THEIR SISTER.

BUT LIKE ALL BLACK WOMEN WHO HAVE HAD TO FACE HARDSHIPS, SHE GATHERED UP HER CHILDREN AND GRANDCHILDREN AND PUSHED FORWARD ALWAYS BELIEVING IN A BETTER DAY TO COME, I LOVED HER WITH ALL MY BEING.

THEIR STORY DOES NOT END THERE, PERCY AND FLORENCE HAD TO ENDURE MANY HARDSHIPS AFTER THE TORNADO.

THE HOUSE THAT THEY HAD LIVED IN WAS COMPLETELY DEMOLISHED, THEIR GARDENS DESTROYED AND THEIR ANIMALS MISSING.

THEY WERE LEFT HOMELESS WITH NOTHING TO THEIR NAME, BUT EACH OTHER AND THE CLOTHES ON THEIR BACKS.

THEY WERE GIVEN SHELTER BY THE FURBERT FAMILY, AND THE FRANCES FAMILY OF HAMILTON PARISH FOR A COUPLE OF DAYS.

REV. L. H GUNNER, FROM THE HOLY TRINITY CHURCH IN BERMUDA IN BALIEY'S BAY RECTOR OF HAMILTON PARISH CAME TO THEIR RESCUE AND WENT ON THE RADIO TO PLEAD FOR HELP FOR THE SMITH FAMILY, AS WELL AS MANY OTHER FAMILIES THAT NEEDED HELP ALSO.

HE WAS ABLE TO RAISE A GOOD BIT OF MONEY, CLOTHING, AND FOOD FOR THE FAMILY. ALL OF HIS GOOD WORK WAS A BLESSING FOR THE SMITH FAMILY.

MR. STUART OUTERBRIDGE, CAME TO THEIR RESCUE AND OFFERED THE SMITH FAMILY A PLACE TO STAY IN BALIEY'S BAY, RENT-FREE FOR AS LONG AS THEY NEEDED IT.

THEY WERE LEFT POOR, BUT THEY HAD EACH OTHER AND WERE A HAPPY FAMILY AND WORKED TOGETHER. THE MONEY THAT REV. GUNNER HAD RAISED AFFORD THEM FOOD CLOTHING AND FURNITURE.

WITH EIGHT CHILDREN AND THREE GRANDCHILDREN, ALL THE HELP THAT THEY RECEIVED WAS GREATLY APPRECIATED.

LIFE SEEMED TO BE GETTING BACK TO SOME KIND OF NORMALCY. PERCY WENT BACK TO THE PROPERTY WHICH HE AND HIS FAMILY HAD LIVED ON FOR MANY YEARS.

HE OFFERED TO BUY THE PROPERTY FROM THE TALBOT'S BUT THEY REFUSE TO SELL IT TO HIM. THAT ANGERED HIM AND CAUSED HIM A GREAT DEAL OF DISTRESS. HE WANTED HIS FAMILY TO HAVE THEIR OWN LAND.

"GOOD ENOUGH TO RENT TO FOR YEARS, BUT NOT GOOD ENOUGH TO BE GIVEN THE OPPORTUNITY TO BUY AND BUILD WEALTH FOR HIS FAMILY".

FOR HE HAD LIVED THROUGH THE TIME WHEN HIS PARENTS HAD THEIR LAND TAKEN FROM THEM IN TUCKER'S TOWN BERMUDA CAUSING HIM AND HIS SIBLINGS TO LOSE OUT ON THEIR BUILDING OF GENERATIONAL WEALTH FOR THEIR FAMILIES.

TO MAKE MATTERS WORSE, THE NEW BOAT THAT HE HAD PURCHASED, WHEN HE WENT TO TOM MOORE'S TAVERN EARLY IN THE MORNING TO SET OUT ON HIS FISHING TRIP, HIS BOAT WAS NOT AT ITS MOORINGS, "WHAT THE F ----K" HIS BOAT WAS MISSING AND NEVER TO BE FOUND.

THAT ALMOST KILLED HIM, HIS LIVELIHOOD WAS GONE "HOW WAS HE TO FEED HIS FAMILY AND PAY HIS BILLS".

LATER HE FOUND OUT THAT THE TALBOT'S HAD SOLD THE PROPERTY TO THE HODGSON FAMILY, WHO WERE THEIR NEIGHBOURS, AND IT CAUSED MORE BAD BLOOD BETWEEN THEM.

IT IS A STORY OF THE HAVES AND THE HAVE NOTS, EVEN IN THE BLACK COMMUNITY.

YOU HAD SOME BLACKS, THAT THOUGHT THEY WERE BETTER THAN THE OTHER AND TURN THEIR NOSES UP AT THEIR POORER NEIGHBORS.

A CLASSIC CASE OF CLASS PREJUDICE IN THE BLACK COMMUNITY, IN THE EARLY DAYS.

PERCY'S LIFE WAS NEVER THE SAME, HE BECAME AN ALCOHOLIC AND WAS VERY BITTER WITH WHAT LIFE HAD DEALT HIM THAT HE COULD NOT GIVE HIS FAMILY THE LIFE THAT HE WANTED FOR THEM.

THIS IS THE STORY OF MANY BLACK MEN IN BERMUDA AT THAT TIME. THEY WERE MADE IMPOTENT BY THE SYSTEM THAT WAS IN PLACE AT THAT TIME. PERCY IN TIME GAVE UP DRINKING AND FOUND PEACE.

FLORENCE ON THE OTHER HAND, WORK HER "ASS OFF" FOR HER FAMILY, ALWAYS STRESSING THE IMPORTANCE OF OWNERSHIP OF PROPERTY.

SOMETHING THAT SHE HAD NEVER KNOWN, BECAUSE OF ALL THE TRIALS AND TRIBULATIONS THAT PERCY AND HER HAD TO ENDURE.

BUT SHE NEVER GAVE UP HOPE, AND HER BELIEF IN A BETTER DAY TO COME FOR HER CHILDREN AND GRANDCHILDREN.

PERCY AND FLORENCE LIVED TO SEE THEIR CHILDREN AND THEIR GRANDCHILDREN HAVE OWNERSHIP OF THEIR PROPERTIES AND MAKE BETTER LIVES FOR THEMSELVES.

ALL DO TO FLORENCE'S TEACHING AND HER TENACITY, TO NEVER GIVE UP HAVING BELIEF IN THAT YOU CAN ACCOMPLISH ANYTHING.

NO MATTER WHAT ADVERSITIES YOU MAY GO THROUGH, THERE IS ALWAYS HOPE AND ALWAYS BELIEVE IN A BETTER DAY TO COME.

Many Mourners At Burial Of Tornado Victim

Continued from Page 1

In addition, he has received several parcels of groceries and articles of girls' clothing. At present, he told The Royal Gazette, he is in need of boys' clothing and bedding.

Much of the money has been earmarked for the family of Mr. Percy E. C. Smith, father of Miss Madeline Smith, Mr. Gunner said. Other families were also in need, he added.

He has secured temporary accommodation for the Smith family through Mr. Stuart Outerbridge, but they needed permanent lodgings.

There are others aiding the needy. Between 75,000 and 100,000 lily heads have been offered to competitors in the Easter Lily Pageant by the E. Worrall Outerbridge Company on the understanding that donations will be given to help people whose homes were damaged in the tornado.

Making this announcement yesterday, Mr. Eugene Outerbridge said that the money donated would be turned over to a committee for disbursement. He said the lilies could be obtained today by those who desired them to

be seen on the North Shore Road last night, however.

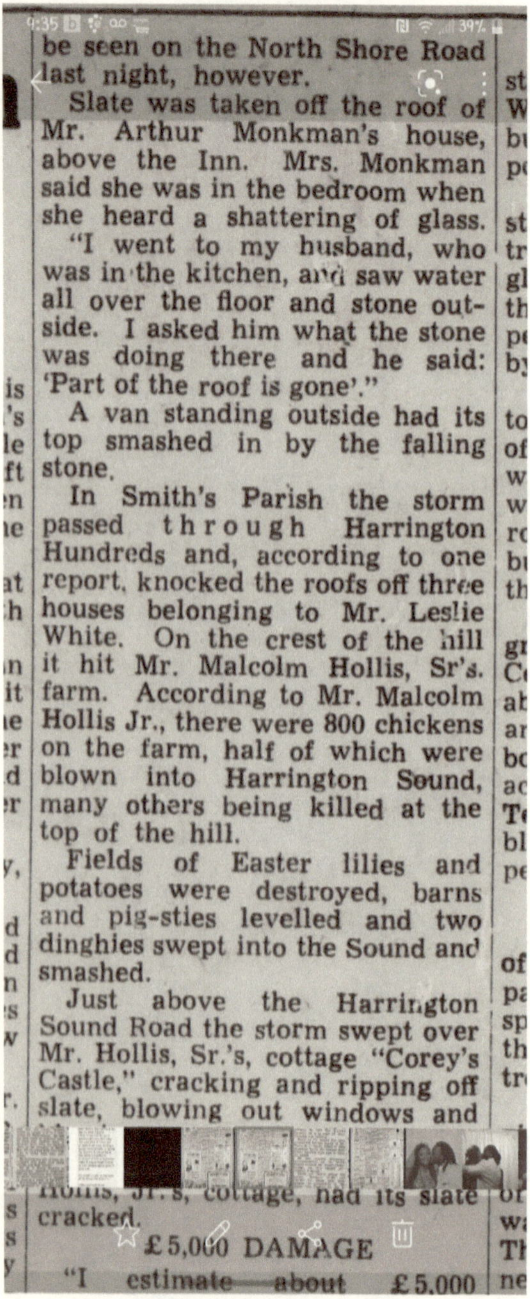

Slate was taken off the roof of Mr. Arthur Monkman's house, above the Inn. Mrs. Monkman said she was in the bedroom when she heard a shattering of glass.

"I went to my husband, who was in the kitchen, and saw water all over the floor and stone outside. I asked him what the stone was doing there and he said: 'Part of the roof is gone'."

A van standing outside had its top smashed in by the falling stone.

In Smith's Parish the storm passed through Harrington Hundreds and, according to one report, knocked the roofs off three houses belonging to Mr. Leslie White. On the crest of the hill it hit Mr. Malcolm Hollis, Sr's. farm. According to Mr. Malcolm Hollis Jr., there were 800 chickens on the farm, half of which were blown into Harrington Sound, many others being killed at the top of the hill.

Fields of Easter lilies and potatoes were destroyed, barns and pig-sties levelled and two dinghies swept into the Sound and smashed.

Just above the Harrington Sound Road the storm swept over Mr. Hollis, Sr.'s, cottage "Corey's Castle," cracking and ripping off slate, blowing out windows and

Hollis, Jr.'s, cottage, had its slate cracked.

£5,000 DAMAGE

"I estimate about £5,000

d from page 1

off. Fortunately Mr. Skinner, his wife and child were at a cousin's house about a quarter a mile away. The child had been left at the house and was to have been picked up at 5.30 p.m., near the time the storm struck.

"I came back and got her at 4.30," Mrs. Skinner said with relief.

The house belongs to Mr. John Soares, who said he only had it insured for fire. Among the lucky ones, Mr. and Mrs. Skinner secured a tarpaulin last night and had it over the house just after dark.

A neighbour, Captain Perry, lost the east end of his roof.

The next victim was old Devonshire Church, which had slate removed from the eastern end of the roof and several panes of glass broken and one window blown out completely.

The Aqua Vista property of Mr. F. J. G. Foote, Kent Avenue, Devonshire, had several of its houses damaged. The roof of Mr. Jack Cousland's house was taken off and several windows blown in. Mr. Charles Oatway lost half the roof off his one-storey house, and another house on the property had a side knocked down and half the roof taken off.

ROAD BLOCKED

Near Lion Rock, on Hamilton Sound, trees were stretched across

bridge, but they needed per-manent lodgings.

There are others aiding the needy. Between 75,000 and 100,000 lily heads have been offered to competitors in the Easter Lily Pageant by the E. Worrall Outerbridge Company on the understanding that donations will be given to help people whose homes were damaged in the tornado.

Making this announcement yesterday, Mr. Eugene Outerbridge said that the money donated would be turned over to a committee for disbursement. He said the lilies could be obtained today by those who desired them to decorate floats from the packing plant of the company at Shelly Bay. He has asked those who wish lilies to bring their own containers.

By making this gift of lilies the company will assist both storm victims and float entries.

Mr. W. R. Evans, Director of Agriculture, reported yesterday that the department had received no direct information of damage to crops as a result of the storm.

Any damage, he thought, would be generally in the Harrington Hundreds area.

He noted that while the heavy rain which accompanied the tornado affected the flowers, Easter lily buds probably received no harm.

Sweeney, 15, died today after a blade from a toy fencing foil pierced his head in an unusual accident.

Truckers from the Corporation of Hamilton, Telephone Company and Electric Light Company sped through the city to repair the damage and clear away fallen trees and wires.

The Bermuda Aviation Services garage on Laffan Street was extensively damaged when part of its rusted corrugated iron roof was lifted off and folded back. The pieces of roofing downed nearby wires to the accompaniment of sparks and flames.

Householders on the street told The Royal Gazette they had constantly petitioned the Corporation for the removal of this building, which they considered to be in a dangerous state of disrepair.

A tree outside the Golden Gate on Reid Street was uprooted, and the broken portions of its trunk stretched across the street. Awnings were ripped from the Bermuda shop, and pieces of building stone on the sidewalk were soon powdered by the feet of those who came to the City to witness the damage. Near the Bermuda Trading Company and A. S. Cooper's shop, broken glass littered the street.

Further up the street, outside the Masonic Hall, a bird's nest had fallen to the ground, and its three 'Easter eggs' were smashed.

vice was found open by a newspaper reporter. Police last night did not disclose whether this had

MONDAY, APRIL 6, 1953

In Southampton there were strong winds and the road near Waterlot Inn was under water, but no serious damage was reported last night from the parish.

In Hamilton last night the streets were littered with rubble, trees, branches, wires and broken glass. Dozens of people were in the streets, checking their property and peering at the damage by torchlight.

The roof of Pearman, Watlington's was torn off, taking a corner of the roof of the Smoke Shop with it. The surrounding area was cordoned off and police rerouted traffic. Workmen were busy with shovels to clear away the debris.

One of Bermuda's most photographed trees, on the corner of Cedar Avenue, was snapped off about three feet above the roots, and its branches, entwined with bougainvillea vine, sprawled across Victoria Street outside the Telephone Company building, blocking all but cyclists or pedestrians.

QUICK REPAIRS

Truckers from the Corporation of Hamilton, Telephone Company and Electric Light Company sped through the city to repair the damage and clear away fallen trees and wires.

The Bermuda Aviation Ser-

Many Mourners At Burial Of Tornado Victim

Yesterday afternoon Miss Madeline Smith, 17 - year - old victim of Sunday's tornado, was buried in Holy Trinity Church graveyard. The graveyard overlooks scenes of destruction wrought by the freak Easter storm which took her life. She was to have been married shortly.

Her weeping family, whose home at Crawl was destroyed, followed her coffin into the Hamilton Parish Church. The sad procession was lead by the Rev. Leslie H. Gunner, rector of the parish.

During the short service Mr. Gunner read a lesson from the fourth and fifth chapters of the second Epistle of St. Paul to the Corinthians, which says: "We have a building of God, an house not made with hands, eternal in the heavens."

Hymns were "Thy way, not mine, O Lord," and "Abide with me." During the service the 23rd Psalm, "The Lord is my Shepherd," was said antiphonally.

At the conclusion of the service the coffin was taken to the grave high on the hillside. The family

second Epistle of St. Paul to the Corinthians, which says: "We have a building of God, an house not made with hands, eternal in the heavens."

Hymns were "Thy way, not mine, O Lord," and "Abide with me." During the service the 23rd Psalm, "The Lord is my Shepherd," was said antiphonally.

At the conclusion of the service the coffin was taken to the grave high on the hillside. The family was led by the mother, who restrained her grief with quiet courage. One sister wept openly, exclaiming: "My poor sister."

The graveyard, which overlooks Harrington Sound, was filled with memorial wreaths placed on the graves for Easter.

Before the service at Holy Trinity Church the Rev. Edward Benjamin held a service in St. John's A.M.E. Church. During the service the hymns "Christ the Lord is risen today" and "My Jesus, I love you," were sung. In his address Mr. Benjamin noted that the Lord moves in mysterious ways.

St. John's Church could not hold all those who came to attend the last rites for the young girl, and the mourners filled Holy Trinity Church.

FUND FOR VICTIMS

More than £300 has been contributed to Mr. Gunner's fund for those in need as a result of the storm, the rector said yesterday.

Continued on Page 2

TRAPPED IN BUILDING

The tornado hit Mrs. Hastings Outerbridge's property, where Mr. Tony Sousa suffered a compound double fracture of the left leg. Mr. Sousa was living in the upper storey of a two-storey building. The tornado levelled the upper storey, and Mr. Sousa fell through to the lower storey and was trapped.

Mr. Morris Cooper, Jr., who was at Mrs. Outerbridge's house when the accident occurred, heard Mr. Sousa calling for help. He wrenched open the large lower doors of the building, extricated Mr. Sousa, and took him to hospital.

Mrs. Outerbridge's house was also damaged.

Damage was severe in Warwick. Mr. Peter Petty told The Royal Gazette that, standing on a hill near "Faraway" Guest House Warwick, he could see roofs off nine or ten houses. Mount Royal guest house was completely de-roofed and tarpaulins had to be put up hurriedly. The section of the roof covering the bar and billiard rooms of the Warwick Workmen's Club was blown off. The roof was taken off the nearby Methodist Chapel and windows smashed. The roofs were taken off three houses on Spring Hill Avenue, Warwick.

FAMILIES EVACUATED

Families were evacuated from a dozen houses on Ord Road. The house owned by Mr. Gilbert Scott and occupied by Mrs. Elise Soares

the roof covering the bar and
billiard rooms of the Warwick
Workmen's Club was blown off.
The roof was taken off the nearby
Methodist Chapel and windows
smashed. The roofs were taken
off three houses on Spring Hill
Avenue, Warwick.

FAMILIES EVACUATED

Families were evacuated from a
dozen houses on Ord Road. The
house owned by Mr. Gilbert Scott
and occupied by Mrs. Elise Soares
was completely deroofed, as were
at least two other adjacent houses.

An old rubber tree in the
grounds of "Bloomfield," near the
entrance on the Middle Road,
Paget, was twisted, and the wall
and entrance pillar in ruins. Tall
palm trees bore one frond each
after the storm had passed.

NOTICE

Will customers please note
that if Radios and Electrical
Appliances left for repair are
not called for within 30 days
they will be sold to defray
expenses.

Pearman, Watlington & Co.

the field."
Pan American had seven flights coming in and going out yesterday and none experienced any trouble. The planes reported thunderstorms and winds about 55 to 100 miles north of Bermuda, but these apparently were quite apart from the purely local storm that caused so much damage in the Colony.

—o—

TAIPEH, Formosa, April 5 (Reuter). — Lieutenant General Leon Johnson, commander of the U.S. continental air force, here on a "familiarisation" trip, today inspected Chinese Nationalist Air Force and defence units. General Johnson, who arrived here yesterday, cancelled a proposed conference with Nationalist Air Force chiefs because of the Easter holiday.

did not disclose whether this had
been done by the wind or by a
thief taking advantage of the
storm.

EAST END SPARED

The freak winds apparently did
not hit as far east as Kindley
Field and St. George's. St.
George's police said last night
that they had received no reports
of damage in the parish.

A Pan American Airways
spokesman said that one of their
flights, a Boeing, fully loaded
with passengers, took off at 6.08
p.m., just about the time when
the wind was at full fury in the
central parishes. The plane took
off on instruments because of the
torrential rain, but encountered
no difficulty because of wind.

"It was blowing, all right," said
the P.A.A. spokesman, "but no
more than it frequently does at
the field."

Pan American had seven flights
coming in and going out yesterday and none experienced any
trouble. The planes reported
thunderstorms and winds about
55 to 100 miles north of Bermuda,
but these apparently were quite
apart from the purely local storm
that caused so much damage in
the Colony.

———o———

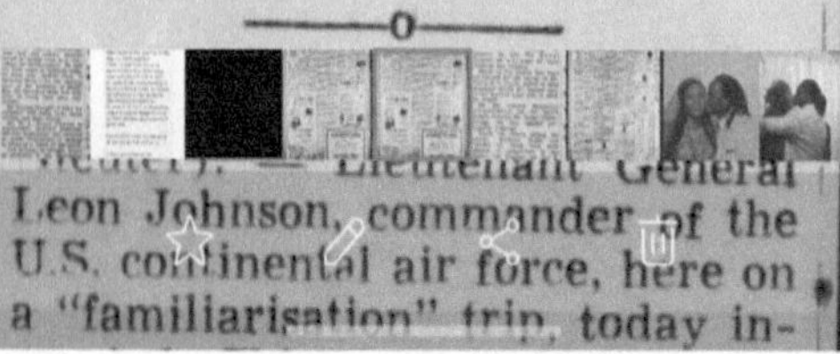

...ieater). Lieutenant General
Leon Johnson, commander of the
U.S. continental air force, here on
a "familiarisation" trip, today in-

Hollis, Jr.'s, cottage, had its slate cracked.

£5,000 DAMAGE

"I estimate about £5,000 damage on that farm," the younger Mr. Hollis observed. No insurance is carried.

Captain Corey, who lives in "Corey's Castle," had his car, parked off the Harrington Sound Road on the sea side, blown overboard.

A convertible taxi, driven by Mr. Sidney DeSilva, was also blown into Harrington Sound. A witness said the wind "lifted the driver out of the car." The wind knocked off the top of the convertible, which perhaps saved Mr. DeSilva's life. He escaped with a cut finger.

The tornado moved across Harrington Sound, severely damaging the home of Mr. Percy Outerbridge, just below Holy Trinity Church. A tree near the Gaiety Theatre was blown down, completely blocking the North Shore Road. It was reported that the roof of the theatre had also been removed.

TRAPPED IN BUILDING

The tornado hit Mrs. Hastings Outerbridge's property, where Mr. Tony Sousa suffered a compound double fracture of the left leg. Mr. Sousa was living in the upper storey of a two-storey

fell through to the lower storey and was trapped.

Mr. Morris Cooper, Jr., who was at Mrs. Outerbridge's house when

Continued f...

direction changed from south-east to north-east, and then suddenly swung back through south to westerly, and the wind decreased to about 15 m.p.h. The excessive wind lasted only a minute or less.

"During the day we recorded a total of 1.82 inches of rain, but we have not yet ascertained how it was distributed over the 24-hour period, although of course most of it fell during the storm."

Most of the damage reported last night was in the central parishes--in Devonshire, Warwick and in the City of Hamilton. The ends of the Island—St. George's and Somerset — apparently escaped altogether.

Two cars were blown into Harrington Sound. The driver of one managed to escape without injury and the other car was parked at the roadside. The cars are resting in shallow water, but not attempts had been made to retrieve them last night, Hamilton Police reported. A car on Cedar

The swath of destruction across Devonshire started somewhere on the south side, hitting the South Shore Road slightly east of the

of glass broken and one window blown out completely.

The Aqua Vista property of Mr. F. J. G. Foote, Kent Avenue, Devonshire, had several of its houses damaged. The roof of Mr. Jack Cousland's house was taken off and several windows blown in. Mr. Charles Oatway lost half the roof off his one-storey house, and another house on the property had a side knocked down and half the roof taken off.

ROAD BLOCKED

Near Lion Rock, on Hamilton Sound, trees were stretched across the road and St. George's to Hamilton buses had to be re-routed.

The tornado went across Devonshire Marsh taking the tin roof off a barn but leaving a pony stabled inside safe.

On the North Shore several houses were damaged above the Clay House Inn. No damage could

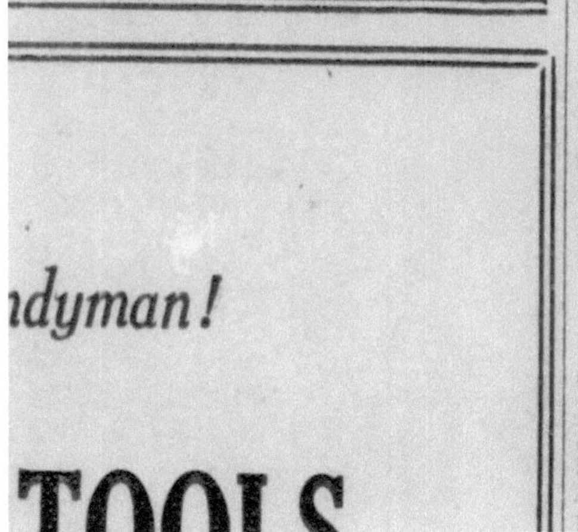

and Somerset — apparently escaped altogether.

Two cars were blown into Harrington Sound. The driver of one managed to escape without injury and the other car was parked at the roadside. The cars are resting in shallow water, but not attempts had been made to retrieve them last night, Hamilton Police reported. A car on Cedar Avenue was blown off the road.

DEVONSHIRE HIT

The swath of destruction across Devonshire started somewhere on the south side, hitting the South Shore Road slightly east of the junction with Tee Street. The wind tore down cedar trees and took the rook off Mr. John Marirea's barn.

The tornado apparently took a diagonal course across Devonshire, and Mr. Ronald Skinner's house, near the Brighton Hill Road, had most of its slate taken

ything . . . .

arpenter And The Har

OWORKING

BOOKS BY AUTHOR

HIS EMINENCE ABUNA YESEHAQ MANDEFRO

WORDS OF INSPIRATIONS AND HOPE

POEMS

BY INTERNATIONAL POET JULIET D WILKINSON, FOUND ON POETRY SOUP.COM

ONE DOCUMENTARY TITLED

WHEN A MAN'S SKIN IS NO MORE SIGNIFICANT THAN THE COLOR OF HIS EYES.

THE EILEEN MARY (TEDDY) BING BASDEN STORY COVERS THE LIFE OF MY FRIEND AND MENTOR, THE LATE TEDDY BING BASDEN FROM THE '50S TO 2000.

FROM THE UNITED KINGDOM TO AFRICA TO BERMUDA AND HER BECOMING ONE OF THE FEW BRAVE CAUCASIAN WOMEN AT THAT TIME TO BECOME A MEMBER OF THE PROGRESSIVE LABOUR PARTY.

WHOSE FIRST HUSBAND, THE LATE QC, GEOFFREY BING WAS INSTRUMENTAL IN HELPING THE PROGRESSIVE LABOUR PARTY IN THE EARLY YEARS SERVING AS AN ADVISOR ON CONSTITUTIONAL LAW, ALSO HE WAS A CONSTITUTIONAL ADVISOR AND ATTORNEY GENERAL OF GHANA, AND A GOOD FRIEND OF THE LATE PRESIDENT KWAME NKRUMAH.

HAS BEEN SHOWN IN GHANA, THE UK, AND ON FRESH TV IN BERMUDA.

"THE DEBT THAT WE OWE TO OUR ANCESTORS
IS A DEBT THAT WE CAN NEVER REPAY."

"LOVE AND FORGIVENESS IS THE KEY TO
ALL HUMANITY BUT THAT DOES NOT
MEAN THAT WE FORGET, HOW CRUEL
MANKIND CAN BE TO EACH OTHER."

"PRAYER, PATIENCE, GRATITUDE,
OPENNESS, AND HUMBLENESS ARE THE
WAYS OF THE SPIRITUAL SEEKER."

www.ingramcontent.com/pod-product-compliance
Lightning Source LLC
Chambersburg PA
CBHW022043050726
47591CB00003B/925